Exploring the Galaxy

Pluto

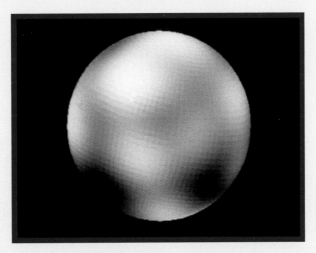

by Thomas K. Adamson

Consulting Editor: Gail Saunders-Smith, Ph.D.

Consultant: James Gerard
Aerospace Education Specialist, NASA
Kennedy Space Center, Florida

Capstone
press

Mankato, Minnesota

Pebble Plus is published by Capstone Press
151 Good Counsel Drive, P.O. Box 669, Mankato, Minnesota 56002
http://www.capstone-press.com

1 2 3 4 5 6 08 07 06 05 04 03

Library of Congress Cataloging-in-Publication Data
Adamson, Thomas K., 1970–
    Pluto / by Thomas K. Adamson.
    p. cm.—(Pebble Plus: exploring the galaxy)
    Summary: Simple text and photographs describe the planet Pluto.
    Includes bibliographical references and index.
    ISBN 0-7368-2116-3 (hardcover)
    1. Pluto (Planet)—Juvenile literature. [1. Pluto (Planet)] I. Title. II. Series.
QB701 .A33 2004
523.48′2—dc21   2002155607

Editorial Credits
Mari C. Schuh, editor; Kia Adams, designer; Alta Schaffer, photo researcher; Eric Kudalis, product planning editor

Photo Credits
Corbis/Roger Ressmeyer, 21
Digital Vision, 5 (Venus)
Index Stock Imagery/RO-MA Stock, 15
NASA, cover, 1, 4 (Pluto), 9 (Pluto), 19, 21 (inset); JPL, 5 (Jupiter); JPL/Caltech, 5 (Uranus)
PhotoDisc Inc., 4 (Neptune), 5 (Mars, Mercury, Earth, Sun, Saturn), 9 (Earth); PhotoDisc Imaging, 7
Photo Researchers Inc./Chris Butler, 11; NASA, 13; John R. Foster, 17

Note to Parents and Teachers

The Exploring the Galaxy series supports national science standards related to earth science. This book describes and illustrates the planet Pluto. The photographs support early readers in understanding the text. The repetition of words and phrases helps early readers learn new words. This book also introduces early readers to subject-specific vocabulary words, which are defined in the Glossary section. Early readers may need assistance to read some words and to use the Table of Contents, Glossary, Read More, Internet Sites, and Index/Word List sections of the book.

Word Count: 125
Early-Intervention Level: 15

Table of Contents

Pluto

Pluto is usually the farthest planet from the Sun. Pluto and the other planets move around the Sun.

Pluto

The Solar System

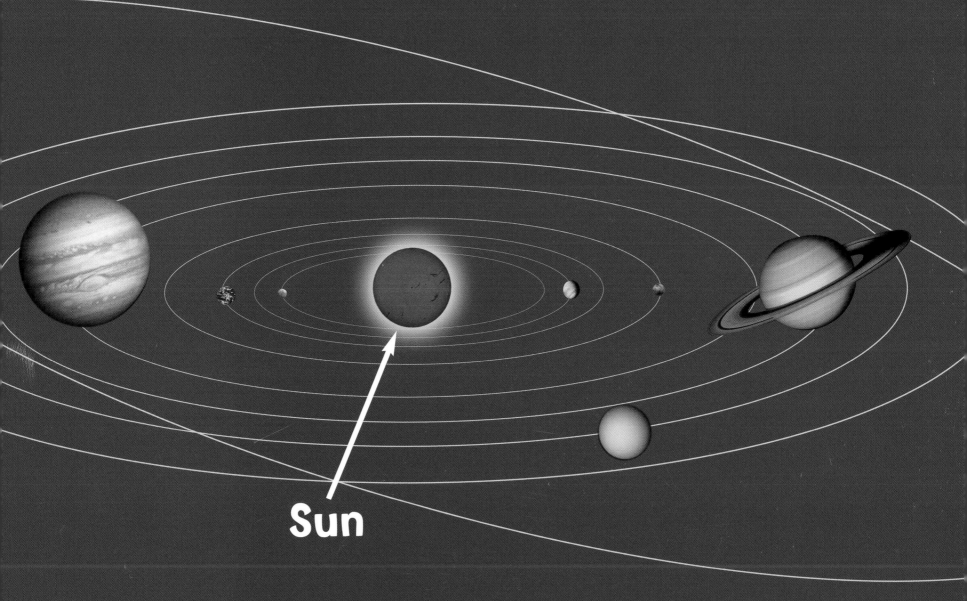

Sun

5

Pluto's Size

Pluto is the smallest planet
in the solar system.

Pluto is shown on the left. Pluto's moon,
Charon, is on the right.

Earth is about five times wider than Pluto. Even Earth's Moon is larger than Pluto.

Earth

Pluto

Pluto's Moon

Charon is Pluto's only moon. Charon is smaller than Pluto.

Features

Scientists do not know much
about Pluto's surface.

Scientists think Pluto is
made of rock and ice.
Pluto may have some craters.

Pluto has a thin layer of air.

The air is usually frozen.

Pluto is very cold.

Pluto's moon, Charon, rises
over Pluto's horizon.

People and Pluto

Scientists plan to send
a spacecraft to Pluto.
The trip will take
about 10 years.

People cannot see Pluto from
Earth without a telescope.
Even through a strong
telescope, Pluto looks
like a fuzzy ball.

Pluto

Glossary

crater—a large bowl-shaped hole in the ground

Earth—the planet we live on

moon—an object that moves around a planet; both Pluto and Earth have one moon.

planet—a large object that moves around the Sun

scientist—a person who studies the world around us

spacecraft—a vehicle that travels in space; spacecraft from Earth have explored every planet except Pluto.

Sun—the star that the planets move around; the Sun provides light and heat to the planets.

surface—the outside or outermost area of something

telescope—a tool people use to look at planets and other objects in space; telescopes make planets and other objects look closer than they really are.

Read More

Goss, Tim. *Uranus, Neptune, and Pluto.* The Universe. Chicago: Heinemann Library, 2003.

Rau, Dana Meachen. *Pluto.* Our Solar System. Compass Point Books, 2003.

Thompson, Luke. *Pluto.* The Library of the Planets. New York: PowerKids Press, 2001.

Vogt, Gregory L. *Pluto.* The Galaxy. Mankato, Minn.: Bridgestone Books, 2000.

Internet Sites

Do you want to find out more about Pluto and the solar system? Let FactHound, our fact-finding hound dog, do the research for you.

Here's how:

1) Visit *http://www.facthound.com*

2) Type in the **Book ID** number: **0736821163**

3) Click on **FETCH IT**.

FactHound will fetch Internet sites picked by our editors just for you!

Index/Word List